INTERNAL
WEST

Books by Priscilla Becker

Internal West
Stories That Listen

INTERNAL WEST

priscilla becker

Carnegie Mellon University Press
Pittsburgh 2022

The author would like to thank the following magazines in which these poems first appeared, some in different forms: *The Paris Review*: "Vertigo," "What They Didn't Know and How It Hurt Them," "The Shadow," "Letter After an Estrangement," "Preparing for Export," and "Overture to an Hallucination"; *Raritan*: "The People in the Picture" and "Make It Like Us".

Cover design by Connie Amoroso

Library of Congress Control Number: 2021947244
ISBN: 978-0-88748-657-9

10 9 8 7 6 5 4 3 2 1

Internal West won *The Paris Review* Prize and was first published by Zoo Press, Lincoln, Nebraska, in 2001.

First Carnegie Mellon University Press Classic Contemporaries Edition, February 2022

Without Whom Never:

Mr. Haas, Mr. Hildreth and his pond, Vladimir Tax, Silky.

Contents

A Note on Priscilla Becker

First of all, to formal matters. The ragged edges and crooked seams of these poems are a deception, a manner of holding something over the mouth to make the voice sound like another instrument altogether. Indeed, nothing *could* be innocent that looks so innocent as all this:

> When I emerge, nobody
> looks like me anymore. Most of all you. Or least.
> Isn't it strange how either one fits?
>
> You can do that with words, use one
> for the other.

The poet has discovered how to orchestrate her voice, and henceforth she is free and clear, or at least the poems are. Heartbreak, like happiness, requires a complex art, and Priscilla Becker's, whereof the lineaments are set forth here, is for all its "naturalness" a cunning mixture of determinations. Frequently she sets oppositions not at odds but at evens, so that "either one fits"; that is her fashion of representing ecstasy, which will do for either case—I mean for happiness or for heartbreak. Not many male poets can do this for themselves, and Harold Bloom reminds me that Rosalind is a separate, even an isolated instance. Certainly hers—or his—is the figure I should choose whereby to identify Ms. Becker within the canon. She has lots to do with all those other miraculous girls: Julia, Viola, Portia, Imogen, but it is Rosalind who has, in prose, the double vision I would tax Becker's poetry with:

> Those that are in extremity of either [melancholy
> or laughing] are abominable fellows, and betray
> themselves to every modern censure, worse than
> drunkards... I had rather have a fool to make me
> merry than experience to make me sad—and to
> travel for it too.

One catches the intonation, no? It remains to see what it does for this poet, once caught. I suspect her title will help us. I spoke of her being "free and clear," and there is something about an *internalized west*, that American speaking voice at home on the range, which nicely defines or at the very least identifies the location of all this "experience to make me sad." Not a matter of boots and buckskins, the costume of cowgirls, but of lighting out for the territory ahead, when the damage done behind her is perceived as loss. Cut and run, those western verbs, are the overmastering actions here, as Priscilla Becker suffers them:

> You could say I didn't feel
> a thing at all. That is just
> the way I am, but wasn't once.

Rosalind in Wyoming, then? But, no, *internalized*, where the meanings are. Read 'em and reap.

—Richard Howard

A.

The Backyard

One day the sky grows up and stops
impressing us with blues and plots
of light. That is how we know
to come inside. The swamp grass
waves itself away. I know the shallows
of the lake like the rats know it, like the weeds.
I may have been cheating on you then.
Sometimes I sit in water until my body turns
to lamb, until I'm certain I have something
to care for. If the streetlights snap off
when I walk beneath them, I'll not need
to know that now, if the stars turn
to other stars. How could you have known
I'd love you much too late and long—
the golden clover yellowed, wild
       mulberry overgrown.

The Futureless Future

It should not surprise you that I hope
to be passed over by reincarnation.

It would not please me to be
a dog or a blade of grass.

I look forward to a cessation of life.

You remind me that I have always wanted
to be something other than myself.

But I have been given enough time here.

I don't know that perfecting my bark
or wriggling my green blade between
a boy's teeth would satisfy me.

You remind me that I have always liked
to put my feet in the dirt.

But would there be something other to do
than follow at your heels or cushion your feet?

Remember I am not particularly loyal.

You remind me that I have always loved
animals. And perhaps it has seemed so
because I have never much liked people.

Although I would, I think, like the part
about the fur coat and the blanket of snow.

I was always so cold here.

The People in the Picture

Like in the children's book we moved—
representationally. Where the yellow blob
stands in for warmth, and we stood
inside the lines of the house, and daisies
would appear from inside the squares
of lawn—or we called them that—
but often the children would paint them
the color of mustard or peas or
overnight. We were all imagination
and mistake, experiment. The sister's

mouth a puncture in the face,
and all the fingers of the hand the same
fat length. And later, little inverted
arcs appeared beneath her sweaters
and her hair flowed out like a string of dulse.
The mother with a mouth like a jagged
blade, but after a few pages,
we forgave her. Always the bare
tree in the yard and that same stale
smudge above the chimney, hovering

with a meaning as much as the people.
The puffed cloud with human features and,
because it was easy, the double curve of gull
stuck, until the pages corrupt, in the sky.
The slash features of the father
X-ing at the brow in black
impossible knots, or following the straight
bone of the finger indicating
where we might beware, beyond the limit
of the page. The smaller sister running

stiffly—every motion a kind of folding—
jack-knifing a twig to the smiling dog.
The whole first book someone forgets
to draw in her mouth. Her haircut
an accident with pinking shears, and eyes
like little stones sunk into a setting.
And the bubbles were our words!
Which sometimes looked like little murders,
false fingerprints, or attempts at erasure,
by pressing harder, drawing blacker.

The Shadow

We were raised to be discreet
and you, I think, were only
hinting when you traced

my body in the grass.
We made a black thing
out of light—without effort.

And your shape on the sand
looks relieved; my face,
a redundancy. And if we

stood a certain way
we could extend our length
of days until it seemed

that we were squinting
or not breathing properly.
I made a picture with my hand,

a monologue of movement,
which did little toward
impressing you. I have been told

that that was then. Sometimes
I think I see you there; so many
nighttimes look like you.

Vertigo

Describe a scene from your daily life.

The sky has come down around us in a shroud.

Use plain language.

It is dark. An old man comes toward me.
He is smoking—no—it is cold out and that is his breath.
He walks a big dog.

Eliminate all adjectives.

Slowly he coughs into his sleeve.

And adverbs.

What could be the reason for my fear
now that he is just a man with a dog?

Think of yourself as a reporter.

I am standing at the intersection of *Blankity* and *Blank*.
The air loses its temperature.
I have often wished for someone to attack me.

*Each time the character wishes, hopes, dreams, imagines,
it robs the action.*

Closing in on me now, his white breath, and a girl
has appeared at the outskirts of my eye.

Do not rely on odd syntax.

Her shoes look like small puppies
helpless at her feet.

*Remember: overusing simile and metaphor
weakens the prose.*

Is it possible, I mean to say, that you are
making a mistake and I am not
the woman you despise?

Speak with authority.

Yesterday on my way home from school
a bat fell out of the sky.

Try to think of an emotion that represents your world.

Often I become sick in social situations.
And also when I am alone.

Archivism

You will want to make me
visible by propping up facts,
constructing a time line with speed bumps
slowing you at puberty, or throwing up
a cautionary flag. A yellow legend
to tap like a vein with your hand.

I was always hoping for some other
sort of life, flung far from the family tree,
the expository body traceless
and collapsed where a child
finds me out by rote: I failed
in history. If you must look there
look. See also this illiterate
violet: it is a gift.

Residual Romanticism

It is only a childish addiction
to drama that makes you call it
death when it is really just
an ordinary broken heart.

And the girl who broke it
has really done nothing
unusual or expert.

It will be hard to come up with
reasons to go on—typically,
there are none; insulting to learn
you now know you're alive.

You already knew.

Now would be a good time for a promise
        to come true.

At night imagine that the world
without you isn't quite the world,
and watch their sorrow like a smoke
follow the far tilted hills.

Adult Themes

That sort of happiness has never much
interested me. It seems too much
like something else, so small
and sharp like a little jewel so
easy to lose. And much of our lives
in its pursuit, planning for it,
coaxing it like a temperamental lover.
And like a temperamental lover,
it coming when it chooses and
leaving that way too. So that
the happiness itself, as other things
too dearly missed, is overwhelmed.

Make It Like Us

When you leave in the morning
me alone with your bird
I think of hurting it, killing it maybe
in some bloodless way.

It is not that the bird reminds me of you.

I remember when I first
got up close and saw its frightening
molten feet you had another name for—
the bird one—but I've forgotten that now.
Its eyes cruel and evasive, and lids
like sleepy guillotines of cooling lead.
I extended a family sort of love—
choiceless and assumptive, and let it
perforate my hand, expressionless.

Back in Africa, or wherever it came from,
there are millions of birds
just like it, crowding the branches,
living authentically, in flocks
or what have you, eating beyond
seeds and freeze-dried pellets,
symbolic of nothing, each one taken
alone, but together some sort of
symphony I'd rather not go into.

But here a song is not enough,
but that it learn to speak.
You stood like a conductor
before its perch, and every sound
said something about us.

The Smile

The words we said don't seem so very
living now and even then, as they were said,
were busy making memory. Some dropped
straight dead from our lips
or hesitated in the air then took a plunge.
It did something to our mouths—
the smile that's a line with stops in it,
like something trained away from curves,
that at the start decides to kill itself,
that sets out aimed for going up
then gets consumed by the rule of the muscle.
The smile is architecture too,
and we don't like the Gothic archway anymore.
We wonder is it living in the lips at all.
Our mouths now in collaboration
with the eyes. I think they try to meet
each other on the sly, so that the lash
descending the eye feels like a kind
of kiss, and lips look like a cold
and borrowed blue. It exited the face.
I'm looking through my pictures
so I can show you what to do.

Snowdonia

Not that the hair is blond,
but that it is not brown.
My mistake.

Not even once to settle
curiosity, or hiding on the legs
beneath my clothes.

The same way a violet
is not really blue and so
can live in two fields at once.

Or more.
Now I think I understand
the litany of jokes—

a visible absence
positioned on my head,
a station in the arc

of vanishing.
Not hard then to imagine
dropping one more notch below

to white, which means a hollow
follicle, a life of exhausting
chameleonism.

See. We're happy again.

Idiom

There is nothing wrong with the mail.
When I think of your city, the streets
hurt. One thing the actor must master
is what to do with the hands.
When we were small listening
to French tapes and making up a French dance:
Hamidou is a boy from Dakar.
When he looks out his window everything flies.
The letters he sends to the girl in Ohio
he sends by bird. Another thing:
speak with the eyes. I will write you
no more letters? The place
for the hands is over the mouth.

The Couple on the Beach

It is not uncommon that the woman
in the white bathing suit is beautiful,
nor that the man is fat and old.
Neither would surprise me—
their tenderness, or their slowly
picking each other to shreds.
But I am going to try not to tell.
I collect stones and I build castles
and I bury myself in the sand.
I am allowed to describe the sea
when they're not in it—solid,
stopped in the middle of a motion,
immense ungiving slab of slate,
it hurts to swim in here.
And then I do a disgusting thing,
I smoke, and snuff the last
unclaimed molecule from the sky.

When the couple leaves, the day
can find no reason to continue.
One person seems too few
to shine the sun for.
With some sadness, I agree to leave
my stones behind.
I am also allowed to mention
the moon when they're not
under it. But they are.
Will you close your eyes too?

September is near, and then
you won't need beaches anymore.
You'll think your bathing suit looked
foolish, what a useless thing, sand.

Preparing for Export

I do not live in Niger, but once
a man begged me to stop living
my life in Long Island City
and come and join him there.
You see my point.
I am a girl of uncommon
inertia. If it weren't for the night,
I'd never leave my bed at all.

You see this life is lived
on the premise that it is worth living it.
Someone said tonight *you can't ignore
the twentieth century.*
Watch me.

That's How I Escaped My Certain Fate

What I like best about the history book
is its simple text, like a translation
from the way we talk into the way we'd like to.
The direct style slashes through hope to fact
and strips our wishy feelings to naked information.
It snubs detail for vivid catastrophe
and puts a light on shadowy nuance,
slurring down the alphabet of rearranged event
until it seems to make sense our ending up at Z.

I often think I see a pattern hung above
the disintegrating pages, like a distillate
of poisons I will ever after avoid.
By the time I turn the page, how the vapors
change their form—crystal sugar
I am powerless to deny.

After that, it's the pictures—the closet door fails
to get its point across. I am locked behind it,
pounding invisibly. The cat's stunned
stoplight eyes glow more succinctly.
Or the sheer education of your injury series—
the time-elapsed bruise reordering
and abridging the spectrum of visible pain.

And here, but for me, a street sucked clean
of people—shaky, lightless, amateur—
somehow captures the feel of sudden
evacuation. As after a warning
I never learned to properly identify.

Influence

If there isn't already there should be
a fairytale about a beautiful girl
who cannot see her own reflection.

A mirror or window or lake divulges
nothing—not shadow, neither absence.
Imagine a green that is green and not

the image of her eyes, the shape
of a winter tree saying nothing about her
though it be angles and sticks

and sensibly grey. Suitors describe
her beauty, draw pictures, invent
compensatory glass, in which she takes

no interest. If she were asked,
and she never is, she would say she looked
very much like a sudden desire.

Heredity

Because they know how the story ends,
they are sad from the beginning.
A mistake is made and they read the script,
an underling is fired.

In the cast of characters, their names
do not appear. But later they are pencilled-in
at the margin and resented by the crew
who likes things the way they were.
Unfortunately for him, his character
is weak, and for her, a room stuffed
with identical hopefuls on the day of the audition—
predictable, humorless, and premature.

Let's break up now, she says on their first date.
And although nothing terrible has quite yet
happened, she plots with the flourescent
stars the moment before her eyelids adjust.
She feels a backwards mimeographed pull
one could almost read reflection in,
holding the shiny pages up to the bulb—
the *structure* of the face, the *overbite*,
the outline of the marble of the eye.

Some of her lines are flat and uninflected,
her voice set to the register of a program
from when she was a small character.
She misses the people who played
her parents—punctual Dot and histrionic
Art. She looks them up, but no one
has ever heard of them.

I am having no fun at all! she pouts
well before her cue—the stiff dry sound
of quickly turning pages. Then, the reputation.

Between scenes, a few loose minutes
of romance in the park—*I hate mimes!*
she blurts. *They're making fun of me!*
And on her birthday, halfway
through the cake, a sugar-grief,
that puts out all the candles with her tears.

His character undergoes a last-minute revision and,
to emphasize his amazing powers of self-
invention, a different actor plays him in each
successive phase—handsome all, asthmatic,
and charmingly elusive. He will go on
to cleaner cities, to write something
small and disparaging about her in his book.

And they know this.
And so their goodbye lacks invention.
She likes to get her pain all done with from the start.

But could she plot herself into a future,
set out in insubordination of the past—
the continuity team fainted on the floor—
and fix those troubled molecules
in frames or sealed-in oggling jars?
Could she erase recycled features
and fingerpaint her face in with those colors
she can't see yet because she never has before?

Take after take of them kissing—the crew
on overturned milk crates, hats in hands.
They get it right the first time,
but it doesn't count—the cameraman
distracted and director in a fit, her make-up
melted to an orange border at the chin,
and him planning a career of continental adulation.
No way to know that *this*, out of all
the moments, is the one to still.

Offered As Further Proof of Your Age

This coliseum floor, teeming
with brown vials of nitroglycerine, this

drab fig for a face, this
sucked-out olive. All the trees

came down in a wind. You have my permission
to take it all back. How your lip falls slack

when you drink too much.
You drink too much. The force of two of us

forgetting all at once. The trees
make their bed in a crush

of flowers. This pill-strewn room, this
catacomb of flax and bran.

Something has carried me
to a place of small inhabitant.

Crumbs of sand suck down my feet.
Must you always be killing something?

Letter After an Estrangement

I forgot to tell you my husband died.
He was in Spain and something strange
happened with alcohol or water.
He loved them both so much.
Which reminds me, do you want to be
cremated or buried? The difference,
if you do not know, is the ghost or the body,

heaven or sex. Also I am planning a trip.
No place special, just somewhere God
has been. Do you have any ideas?
From there I will bring back vials of Ambergris.
Did I mention I am carrying his baby?
I am in the tenth month and still
he does not show. The house hates me

and breaks everything I touch.
I myself prefer to be left face up
in a ditch and for someone to go to jail
because of what he's done to me.
That way I can watch the stars as they move
to the end of the sky and he can plan his last
meal or some other consolation.

Reformed Cloud Watcher

It would probably hurt to tell you now
I pretended about clouds.

It's funny how the same thing seen
two separate times can do a kind of trick,
as if our eyes could see so many ways
or we ourselves were never twice the same.

There is no other way to say
the thing I wanted never was.
I wasn't fooled or told a lie.

I think it's truth to tell I love
before now more than then, a little
cruel to watch them now.

I wish they did not move at all.

The Snow Globe Girl

He used the real snow
as his mold and shrunk
the flakes and yes made each

exactly alike. He packed her down
and rolled her little head
between his fingers. He kept

the rooms extremely cold.
When he attached her rainbow-
sprinkle buttons, she came

to chilly life. She knew nothing
but the blurred convex home
so found it beautiful,

and dome of plastic sky.
There were the two kinds of weather:
weeks of shocked white frozen limbo,

then the violent inversion—all the ice
rushing to her head and the confusion
and relief of squall.

When the last perfect flake settles
and the northern arc clears
low and home, you can see this girl

replaced to deeper distances.
Each corner of the curve a tentative
horizon, as if it had been blown.

From the Temporal Collection

I can no longer remember
if it was the man on the boat
or the boat. But often there is a portion
of this feeling dusted off and pulsing
lowly when I pass you in the street.
Please understand that when I say you
I might mean a number of things.

though the intrigue that it generates makes me feel
intriguing and the little singeing feeling
a distant relation to a closer connection
that leaves a warm sort of missing,
a general feeling. It will come
as no surprise that we are mostly
made of this. But you don't have to take me
at my word. Just close your eyes
and try to picture someone else.

What They Didn't Know and How It Hurt Them

They tried to hide the body
but a foot kept sticking out the trunk
or arm fell from the rafters.
Strands of hair pushed through the floorboards,
and once the whole corpse
came late to a party.

They were guilty of nothing
or not much: it died all on its own.
But the smell was embarrassing
and they didn't want to ruin
all the fun everybody said they were having
          all the time.

So they dragged it home and burned it,
as if it didn't have a soul.

Species Identification

I suppose it was the plastic
duck at the border of the tub
that kept me there that day
like a yellow leaden anchor.
The frozen face and body
clean of gender, the two black
dots for eyes from which his scream
escapes. The painted changeless
features seemed to be my crass
hypnosis and I stayed in dumb
communion with my bird—
beyond the molded
sculpture of my hair, way past
warmth—until the sky blacked-in
the window and the moon
threw down a little yellow glow.
The duck he was not warm or vocal,
really nothing like a duck at all—
downless and deflatable
with wings that will not
let go from his sides. Held
in shameless captivation, lacking
sense to leave when his kind
took, in synchronized formation,
to the skies. Not failure then
of love, this nesting in cold
fixture, but of instinct only,
to locate, in successive
elsewhere, the sun.

The Sandgirl's Implicit Death

I have always envied those diseases
affecting equilibrium—vertigo, delirium,
romance. You may imagine I've had
my trouble with drugs. Well after fashion,
long past the body's usual resilience,
sand was my drug of choice.
Never particularly liking challenges,
it was available. Only stars,
as it goes, outnumber it. Taking it straight
through the mouth, purity was never
my illusion—bugs and grass
and nicks of glass expected.

Mine was a quiet event, a gentle valvic
shutting. Of course, an inquisition
was done on my body. Grain by grain,
they sifted through my failed and silent piping
with its indelicate imprint of biography.
Following the legend of the years,
their fingers stopped to probe some deep
event or break apart a gnarled accumulate.

The trouble, they found, was with my heart—
having lived so long as metaphor,
neglecting the duties of the purely
physical, it is possible to go too far,
to slip into the plots between the lines
and lie open to interpretation,
to just stay high.

Was it lovely to be imbued with meaning,
to echo down the chambers of the heart,
calling to mind tragic historical lovers,
to count among their lot?
My decline was unremarkable.
First I lost my job, then the love
of certain pivotal persons.
I got confused among the symbols—
this X may just as well be poison,
or if green is the one for *go*.
And sand sifting down the hour,
does that add or take away?

The heart means love. The heart
is a muscle. The heart holds
blood. Its colors are pink
or red. It runs, it pumps,
it is glad. It can break
and break. It can be
young or old, quick or slow,
big or small, the heart can grow
and grow. It bleeds, it shuts,
it speeds. There is a small one
on the hand somewhere.

Obscure Reference

I too have a life to the side.
And while you have taken
a second home, an extra
wife, I have neither one of these
to replicate. I do not need
to travel to a distant place
although I think I go as far
away. And while you lie to her
and her, are absent many days
on business trips, I do
what my economy permits.

I find the world illiterate of faces.
Which may be a kindness,
or at least may look like one.
It may sound that I'm congenial
to your means. But sounds and
images are what I'm speaking of.

Fixed Weather

The way the neon sign lights up
my face tonight makes me feel
foolish and obvious.

But it would be worse I think
to move, to admit along my nerves
something else to occupy.

When there is none.

It is not a lack of will,
but an extra sort of gravity
that I'm accustomed to.

I know it hurts to find me here
like a sudden drop in temperature.

Odd, I know, to find these patterns
lit across my face—
an unreliable glow—

Which will remind you of an emotion.
Or at least that is my hope.

Lines Composed While

Sometimes I cannot tell why we have it,
it seems to do with me all unintended things,
to open some interior dimension, to point out
further distances and leave me artificially alone.

And although the face is generally straight
please don't think that I don't know
the numbers and levels of failures
           in me it indicates.

And all the closeness it is said to bring
is about as close as art to the original thing.

And so for me it is enough for you
to think that by your skill and owing
to our secret thing I've been transported
to a deeper realm and that my eyes
are glassed into a firmer meld or that
my silence is illustrative of feelings felt.

The Dead Soul

One cannot be sure it is invisible.
Perhaps people are just being polite.
And certainly sometimes they stare
just past your shoulder with mouths
halted at the start of speech.
It could be they are looking into the eyes of it,
like an extra black head so ugly
no one has ever had the heart to mention it.

Perhaps it holds its shrunken finger
to its shrivelled lips and pleads
with its eyes no longer jewels or pools—
blank mirrors—of no describable color,
unable to make a shape out of light.

It could be doing anything back there,
hovering like the shadow of your skull—
practicing its black vampiric rituals,
humming dirges, stockpiling its images
from the other world, poised to present them
as historics when your eyelids slip.

Also there is the fact of the burying
weight of it which makes you drag your feet
and allow extra time for everything
or fall asleep or want to. And the sense
that you are never alone, but that half
your feelings are being felt somewhere else—
in a webby lower attic.
Sometimes you look for extra forms
in mirrors. You touch, like a large
flightless bird, the reflection in the window
and are startled by its coldness.

You try foolishly to give it the slip,
ducking into traffic or staying on the bus
into unknown parts of town,
pitching yourself over barricades
or standing hapless behind buildings
granting dumb permission to shadows.

And still, it never makes you feel much less
alone. It trails like a wind-down toy
expecting the free transport you give.
You forget you are eating and leave
a dome of peas and a complacent
fig out for it on your plate.
If you didn't show such respect for the dead,
it couldn't go on living like this.

A Small Accident

It is not true that all children
can draw. I could not draw.
I know because I have found, now,
my drawings in the cellar of the old house.

It was kind of my parents to keep them.
They keep everything.

I didn't show you, although I lit
my hair on fire striking a match
when someone turned the light off
from the top of the stairs.

Like in my drawings, the heads
scratched over with lead,
you would not necessarily know
someone was there.

B.

Much Later and Very Far Away

I am used to more violent extraction
and so at first I almost didn't miss
a thing or quite remember it.

There wasn't any switch—no darkness
where a light had been or chill
recoil where once was sun.

I was never much for either one.

You could say I didn't feel
a thing at all. That is just
the way I am, but wasn't once.

Foreverness

Then, as though the sound had been erased,
I had to call you by your given name.

Or as a town deported sleeping behind
another person's face.

And even yesterday is further
than the sun will indicate.

And memory a travelling thing
occurring in a wrongful place.

Then an early summer feeling
staring off the porch and out of view.

Like packing a bag
for all the long etcetera.

Until Such Time As

I think you must be dead by now,
although I've stopped checking the papers
and keeping always one ear to the ground.

And sometimes a face will lose its name
or word replace a figure or a feeling.

And I don't think I look so long
down corridors and avenues
at backs of heads, retreating shoes,
or hold my finger in the air
as though I were meaning to say.

Also I don't torture myself with talk
and pictures and calling it to mind.

It is a kind of middle feeling
like evening
from a train.

Overture to an Hallucination

Six years have gone since I have been loved
by you. All appearances have been more or less
phantom. There is a boy now applying for your job.
He does not know this. Nor does he know how narrowly
he fills your ghost.

December and the trees are clinging to their leaves.
Here we are, season number five, like the exposed
under-science of a wish. Already I can feel myself
wasting this for sure, molding in my overcoats,
curling up my onion-skin

edges like nails from their estranging
beds, desiccating under long johns, hibernating
in my layered look. When I emerge, nobody looks
like me anymore. Most of all you. Or least.
Isn't it strange how either one fits?

You can do that with words, use one
for the other.

Return

So we were wrong about the future
because I think this is it and it's like
nothing we ever said or thought.

A patient creeping accompaniment
like the subtle stalking accustomed hum.

In pictures we would always say
we looked nothing like that.
And that is something how it feels—inaccurate.

There have been times, although not
several—perhaps you remember one—
a sudden covered waking
late in the day.

Him with Her

I probably will not love you anymore
after tonight. Or I will but without hope.

I think there is a word for this
although I cannot call it back.

It will be a little more like reading
and less the sounds expressed.

Or like a wave pulled back inside
the hand and caught against the skin.

Verisimilitude

I saw you in the park but didn't
say. I started to stop as though
before, it was natural. But then,
as though slapped, I felt it
suddenly turn after. An expression
I could not if asked replicate
assembled on my face—
something close to nonchalance,
which I have never felt.
And in that second that cannot be
further split, I knew you'd see me too—
you were standing in the middle
of the path, watching a scene
I was soon to pass through.
It must have seemed to you
that I continued on my way.

Later Still

I didn't do it so that you'd lose
your way or come alone across
the awful influence of spring.

It was not my voice that formed
inside my throat, but some strange
dialect of truth that made her say.

And it was funnier than it felt.

The streets seemed clay
and some new inward season
spoke in thin destructive petals.

Although you tried to memorize
my hand as an accessory or freeze it
in its naked spiral speaking,
it was the *way* you'd have to trace.

As if tomorrow would be not at all
the same, we stood a little
outside. And waited.

Internal West

Just yesterday I did not know
I had no reason to go on.

For instance, I heard bells.

It's been so long since I heard
bells, I thought at first
I heard them wrong.

Then just as odd a feeling
fell across my heart.

Later, but yesterday still,
a boy dropped his hands
        to his sides.

By way of ending, I thought.

And as I looked they seemed then
to have nothing more to do.

The afternoon and feeling
        in me grew.

Meaning—*today*.

Things I Have Decided Since

Much of what we brought we didn't need.
And the water wasn't really close.
I tried to lose you in the Mato Grosso jungle
but screamed when it got cold.
You stroked my forehead until you fell asleep
and I thought how horrible it would be
to hurt you, what an awful person I would be.
The grey interior hush of the body,
belly slid in slack exotic pleasure,
mouth a soft dent, and deep secluded
shudder, the terrible peaceful blindness,
and inward folded senses, as after a visitor.
It was darker than the pictures.
You were dreaming of before you knew me.

A.

The Horizon at the End of the Bed

I must have looked like some old
artifact etched into the sheet,
some old surrender taken
out of context. And afterall
what I was set to do
I could have managed all alone.

You might remember noticing
by chance in early spring the low
neglected violet hovering
when looking up from some
important gravity and felt
an opening, a way to say farewell.

Late Summer Express and Star

Document this: the boy stinking
of beer and barbecue sauce, tracing
black hearts in the sand. Write it down.
In some official way, take note. And although
he is very young, it hurts him to have
so much time. Under normal circumstances,
he is not one for freckles. Nevertheless,

this happened. In water she sinks
like a man in his boots. She puts her hands out
like a mime assuming a wall.
There is the usual evidence of romance:
opaline harbor lights, the fuzzed stars,
a tiny rivulet of blood on the boy's thigh.
Remember this. You will need to know it later.

All season they lie together on the shore
watching boats collide. The girl is prone
to distraction. The plates drop from her hands
like fish and half-things lie in piles from here
to the end of here. Dead birds seem to collect
in the gullies of her father's summer home
and summer makes her half-discard herself.

Perhaps she loves the boy too much.
Perhaps the father is too permissive.
The old man turning the rusted spokes
of the ferris wheel sees nothing.
Afterall, he is half-blind with alcohol
always on his breath. Prepare yourself
for what is said. The lopish notes of the calliope

could drown a scream. He counts
backwards from ten until his mouth dries
white with spit. Off the record, there is no
scream—some sort of gasp perhaps, some
compliant *no*. By now the boy is very far away,
sick on a train off the Costa Brava.
There may be pieces of her hair elaborately

tucked in his boot, smear of shell-colored lipstick,
ear to hollow of throat. Perhaps she is sorry.
She might well be sorry. In such cases,
you will come to find out, there is never
            an audible cry.

June

Because you loved two things
at once, something invisible and like
a clock has begun to inch toward
its shrill presumption: that we wanted this.

Through with our shabby rainy season,
another one is ushered in.
Only an expression—
no one welcomed it at all.

Something like an April I think
would do. We thought perhaps
that we could falter and fail
to choose. I had assumed

I'd picked up something of your grace
or that a piece of this would keep me
company—perhaps the longest
day? As far as I can tell

this isn't true. I was not prepared
for what occurred, although I'd thought
so often of the end, and wait
and wait for your return.

Blond, Ash

Collapsed on a bench in the park
a boy poked me with a stick
    just to be sure.
The dog was running wild and
the river was being pushed around
by boats. Three women spoke in code
about me. It didn't feel like
heat anymore but that parts
of me were melting.
    Soon the boy
matched me to the dog by our coats.
And for no reason that I know,
I lied.
    The boy pretended
to be called from far off
and the dog seemed not to
recognize my voice.

Autobiography

When I was a child
I was good at grammar.
I have forgotten all that
now. Although I remember

the exercises in books
urging a well-placed
modifier and using boys'
and girls' names like our own.

Always there was a dog
and a pleasant excursion
into the woods or helpful
bit about safety.

And here I am, re-parsing
simple sentences: Henry
loves to read. He has a yellow
dog. Look, he has begun to cry!

Formal Consideration

A lot is made over whether
a leaving person looks back
when he does or just does.
Whether the head swivels
to the side or eyes follow
the clear spot where he lately
was, whether the hand trails
behind. And also if something goes
unreturned such as a sweater or dish—
finding perhaps a disembodied hair.

I do not mean to be
trivial or difficult when afterall
my trouble seems mostly stylistic—
a flourish or an after-gloss,
a director's touch.

And I would hate to feel
so frivolous as this, for wanting
some concern over not only
the end but how it's done.

Even Later

Far away from what you now feel,
and it is hard to say if it is

time I'd like to indicate or
place, will be a sense unlike

the string you may be mid-
acquiring and also nothing like

its sum but, how can I express,
something like the end without

the edge, although with nothing
left unfelt and also no need

for it to be like any feeling else.

Before I Go

I hate the clock by the bed with the long
second hand which does not pulse but runs
in one continuous motion. It was probably felt
that this would disturb less than the usual
tick or blink. Perhaps it was also assumed
that it would go by unnoticed entirely.

Yet there is something horrifying about it,
some kind of precious subtlety, something
repressed and sinister, something swallowed
yet whole. I despise the ticking kind too,
the aloof hypnotic perfection, the bloodless
mimic of the heart. *I love you.*

If You Think It Takes Longer

These twisted trees so like
your body, and artificial light
so like your eyes, you may not

trust this as a compliment.
I did not mean to be here so long
or ever at night. I never knew

that clouds could look so much
like the hood of the world, and cold
buildings begin to glow

like cement-enclosed unstoppable
hearts. You may have tried to warn me
these bare sticks could make me

warm enough, and lamps put on
a version of what shone. It could be
I'm that unloyal, or I went out

oddly trackless in the snow.
I asked myself at slowly slower
interval. What I mean is I am home.

Titles in the Carnegie Mellon University Press Classic Contemporaries Series 1989-2022

Carl Adamshick
Saint Friend

Jon Anderson
In Sepia
Death & Friends

Peter Balakian
Sad Days of Light

Aliki Barnstone
Madly in Love

Priscilla Becker
Internal West

Marvin Bell
The Escape into You
Stars Which See, Stars Which Do Not See

Catherine Bowman
1-800-Hot-Ribs

Michael Casey
Obscenities

Cyrus Cassells
The Mud Actor

Kelly Cherry
Lovers and Agnostics
Relativity

Andrei Codrescu
License to Carry a Gun

Peter Cooley
The Van Gogh Notebook

James Cummins
The Whole Truth

Deborah Digges
Vesper Sparrows

Stuart Dischell
Good Hope Road

Gregory Djanikian
Falling Deeply into America

Stephen Dobyns
Black Dog, Red Dog

Rita Dove
Museum
The Yellow House on the Corner

Norman Dubie
Alehouse Sonnets

Stephen Dunn
Full of Lust and Good Usage
Not Dancing

Stuart Dybek
Brass Knuckles

Cornelius Eady
Victims of the Latest Dance Craze
You Don't Miss Your Water
The Autobiography of a Jukebox

Peter Everwine
Collecting the Animals

Annie Finch
Eve

Maria Flook
Reckless Wedding

Charles Fort
Town Clock Burning

Tess Gallagher
Instructions to the Double

Brendan Galvin
Early Returns

Carol Muske
Skylight

William Olsen
*The Hand of God and a Few Bright
     Flowers*

Dzvinia Orlowsky
A Handful of Bees

Gregory Orr
Burning the Empty Nests

Greg Pape
Black Branches

Joyce Peseroff
The Hardness Scale

Deborah Pope
Fanatic Heart

Kevin Prufer
The Finger Bone

William Pitt Root
The Storm and Other Poems

Mary Ruefle
Cold Pluto
The Adamant

Ira Sadoff
Palm Reading in Winter

Jeannine Savard
Snow Water Cove

Gladys Schmitt
Sonnets for an Analyst

Tim Seibles
Body Moves

Dennis Schmitz
We Weep for Our Strangeness

Jane Shore
The Minute Hand
Eye Level

Dave Smith
The Fisherman's Whore
In the House of the Judge

Elizabeth Spires
Swan's Island

Kim Stafford
*A Thousand Friends of Rain: New and
     Selected Poems 1976-1998*

Maura Stanton
Snow on Snow
Cries of Swimmers

Gerald Stern
Lucky Life
Two Long Poems
The Red Coal

James Tate
The Oblivion Ha-Ha
Absences

Jean Valentine
Pilgrims

Ellen Bryant Voigt
The Forces of Plenty
The Lotus Flowers

James Welch
Riding the Earthboy 40

Evan Zimroth
Giselle Considers Her Future